SUSAN EH THOMAS
ADULT COLORING
HUE KNEW? Series
USING THE POWER AND PSYCHOLOGY OF COLOR TO HEAL & DESTRESS

"Exciting Opportunities"

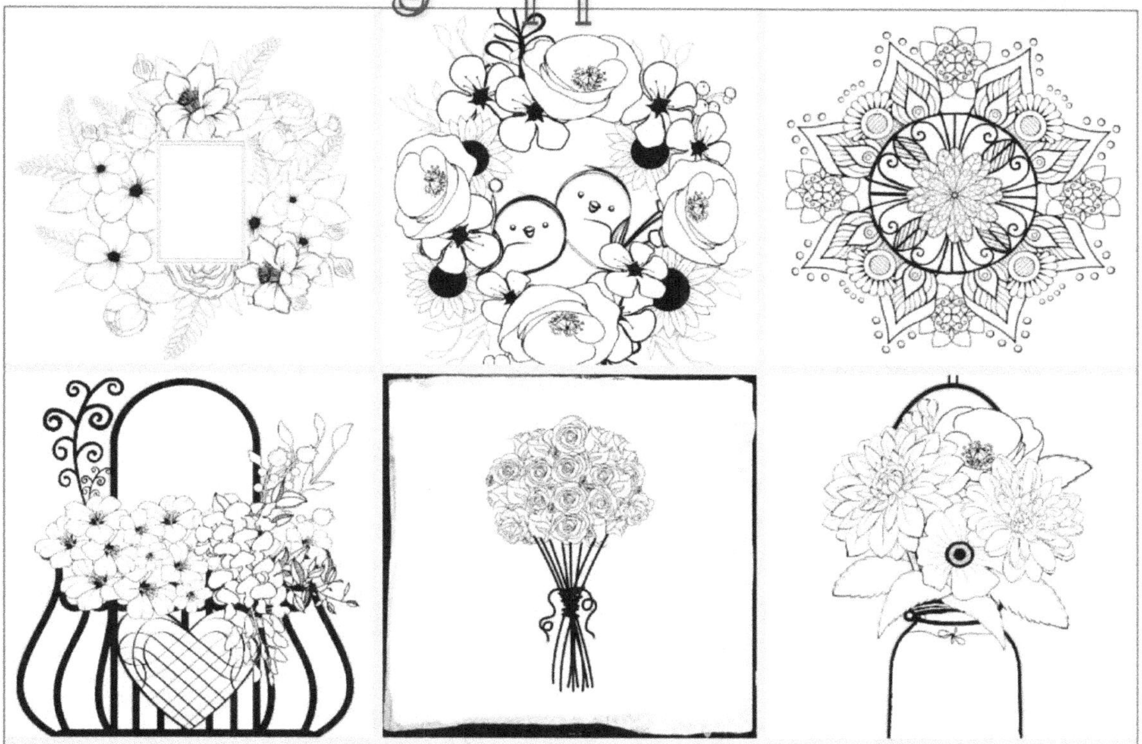

WWW.YOURADVOKIT.COM

Published by YourAdvoKit Publishing
Maryland, USA
Email: susan@youradvokit.com
www.YourAdvoKit.com

Copyright © 2017 by Susan EH Thomas
All rights reserved. No part of this publication
may be reproduced, stored in a retrieval system, or transmitted, in any or any means, electronic,
mechanical, photocopying, recording or otherwise, without prior permission from the author.

A whopping 74% of the population is stressed out. And most all of us want to find relief but don't know how. Or know how, but are too embarrassed, or don't have the time, or worst-case scenario, we don't have the emotional energy to put forth the effort. It's a double edge sword, a dangerous cycle, a dead end.

What - Do - You - Do?

You take baby steps, you take one small bite at a time. And with each bite digested, every ounce of courage gained...you grab another piece of freedom, faith, accomplishment and then you take another bite.

Listen, this coloring book isn't going to radically change your life, or even solve your worst problems...but it is a really good tool to have in your mental health toolbox. And you can never have too many of those.

What separates the "Hue Knew?" series from most other adult coloring books?

Each coloring book comes with a suggested color scheme. These are the colors chosen that work best with the topic of the book [Gratitude, Exciting Opportunities, Positive Thinking.] All colors have certain meanings **and** they all spark or avert certain emotions. I've applied the science behind the color [aka color psychology] and incorporated it into the drawing on the page; giving you the fullest, positive emotional effect.

Of course, you're not held prisoner to these color choices. And can color them whatever hue makes you most happy. After all, isn't that the [colored pencil] point? At the end of the day, for most people who are drawn to coloring books – are seeking a resemblance of peace and a sliver of joy.

Directions: It's okay to go outside the recommended color scheme. But using the colors suggested pre<u>domina</u>tely and **variations of** throughout your coloring sheet best triggers the emotions they're associated with.

BTW: Other than the psychology of color, there's not a lot of difference between me and all the other wonderful coloring books sold online and off, today. I've never viewed myself, or these books as a "competition" because at the end of the day the coloring book for adults is extremely therapeutic.

I'm honored to stand amongst a<u>l</u>l Adult Coloring Book Authors and encourage you to partake in a variety of these books - as we all have a little something different and unique to offer. And you shouldn't put all your eggs in one basket – or rather, in this case – colored pencils to just one brand of coloring pages!

Color Swatch for "Exciting Opportunities"
Orange | Purple
[To view the swatch in color online go to YourAdvoKit.com/HKO.html]

The colors orange and purple create an open mindset, clearing the path for unlimited opportunities. You're better able to explore all options, take decisive action and seize the opportunities that benefit you most. The open mindset leads to a healthy self-confidence and when you have confidence, the world is your oyster. Now "seize the day" is your mantra and you are no longer letting fear stand in your way, rather grabbing exciting opportunities with all the gusto you've got!

Remember; you're not married to using only these colors. You can use variations of and/or move outside of this color palette all together. But to get the fullest "Hue Knew?" effect, try and use the colors suggested [and variations of] predominately. If you're coloring the pages for pure pleasure…then throw the color scheme out the proverbial window and color your world whatever hue makes you happiest!

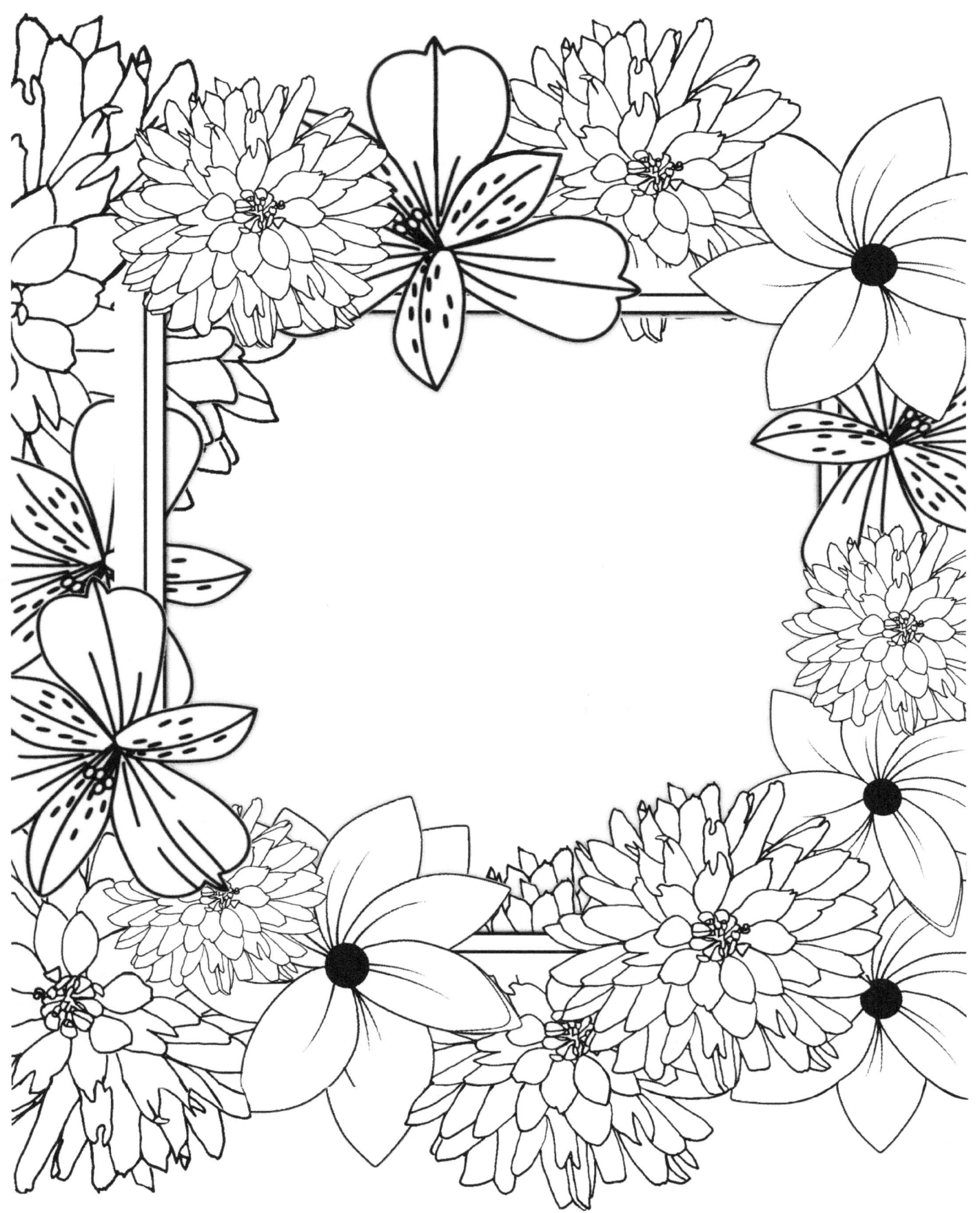

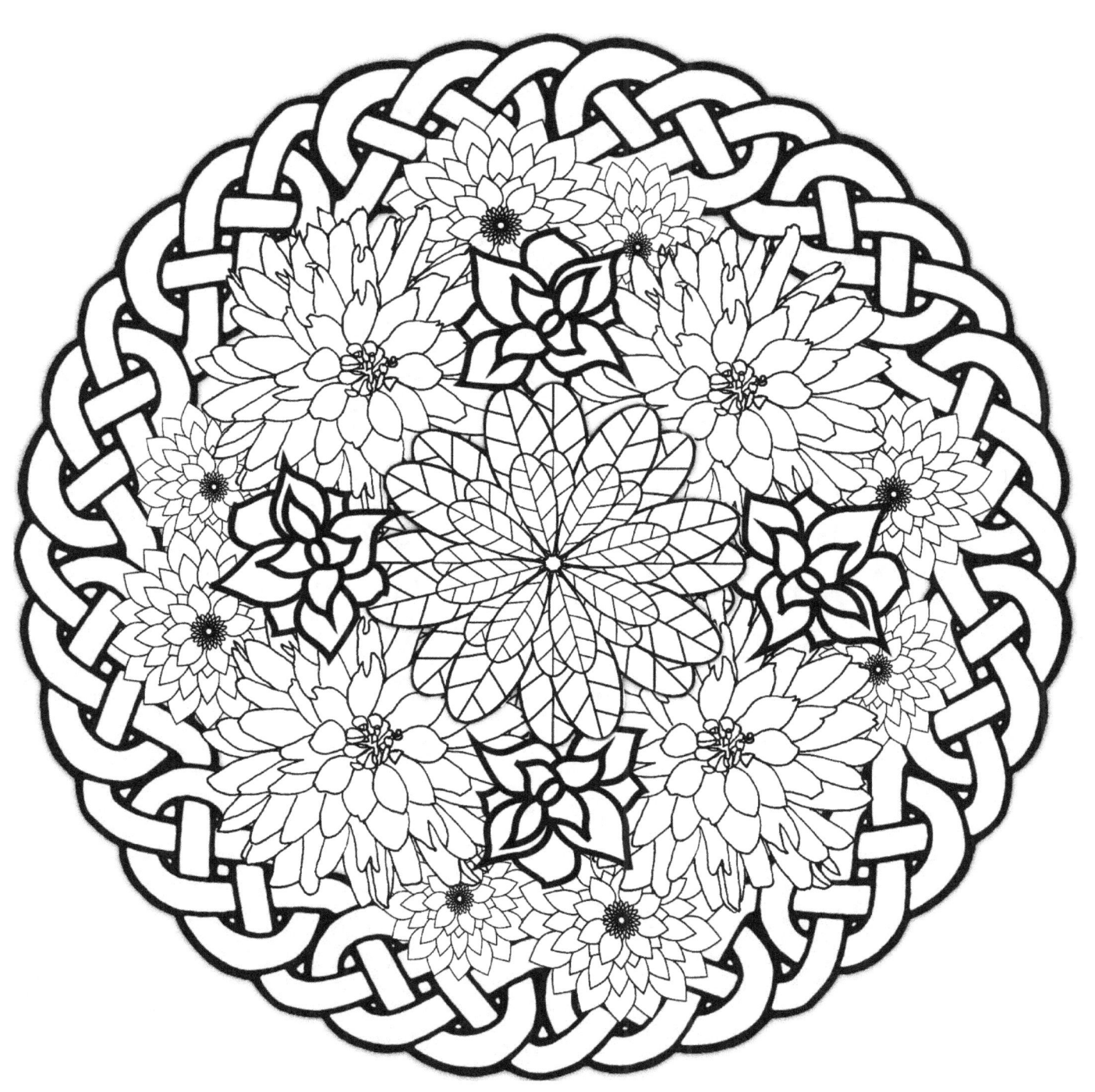

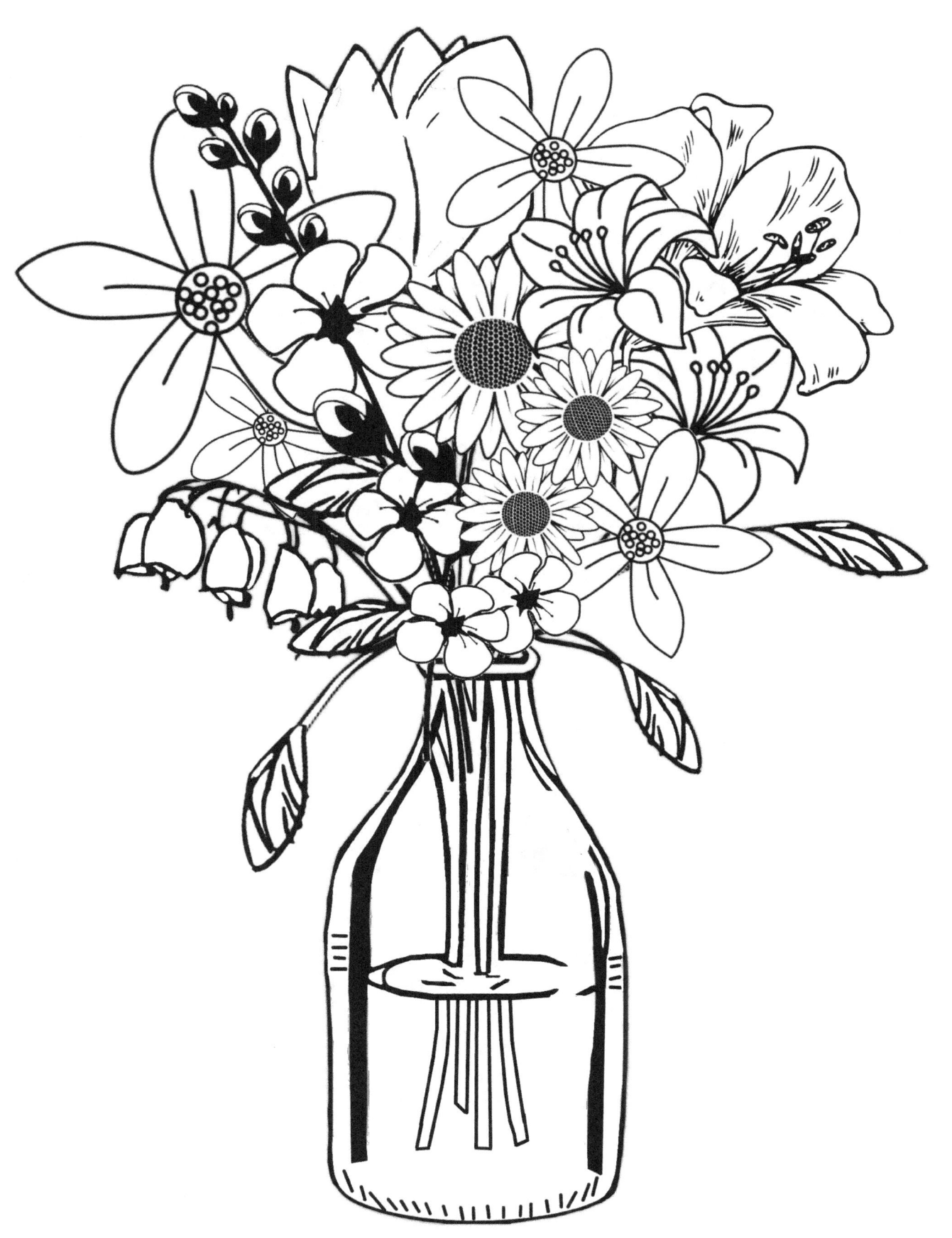

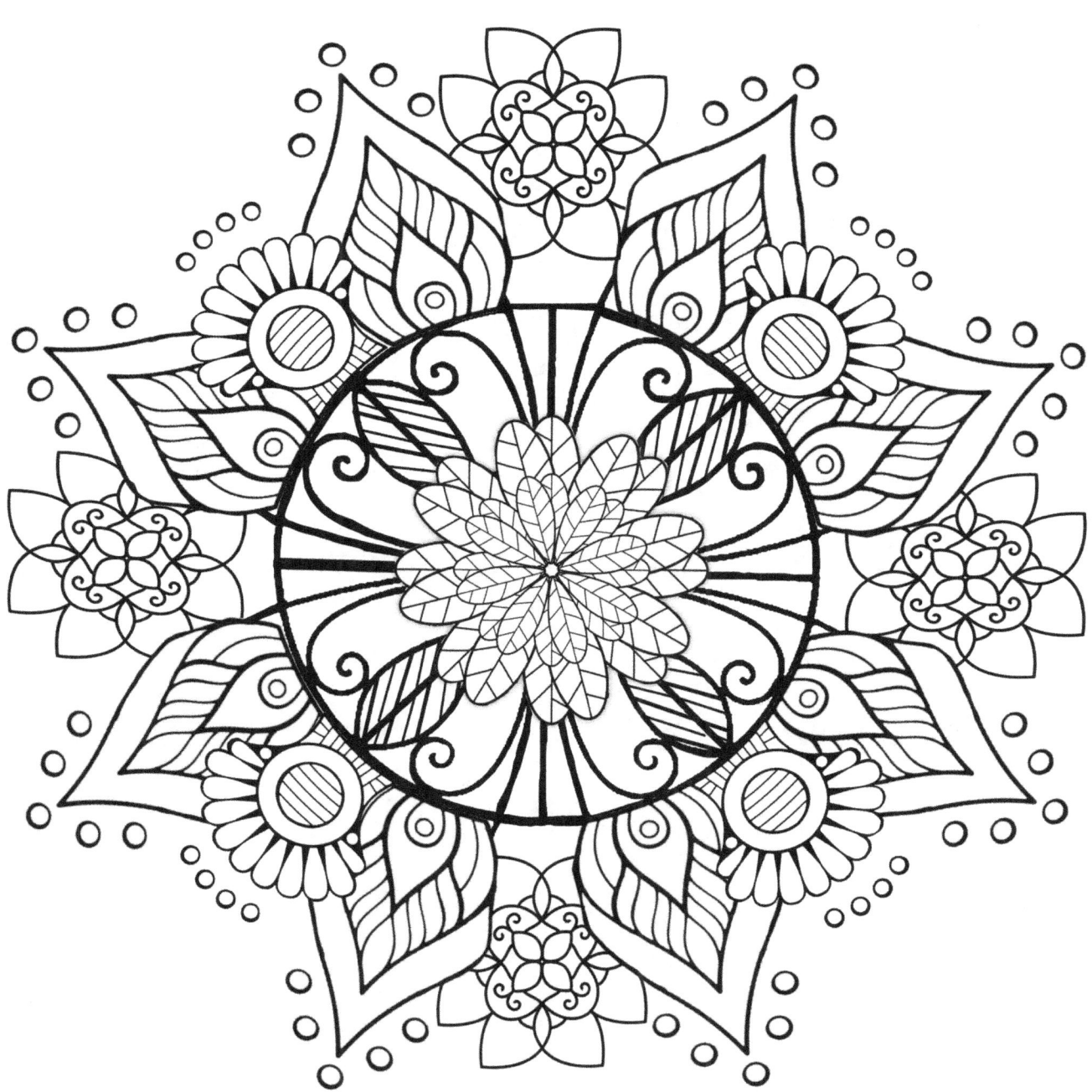

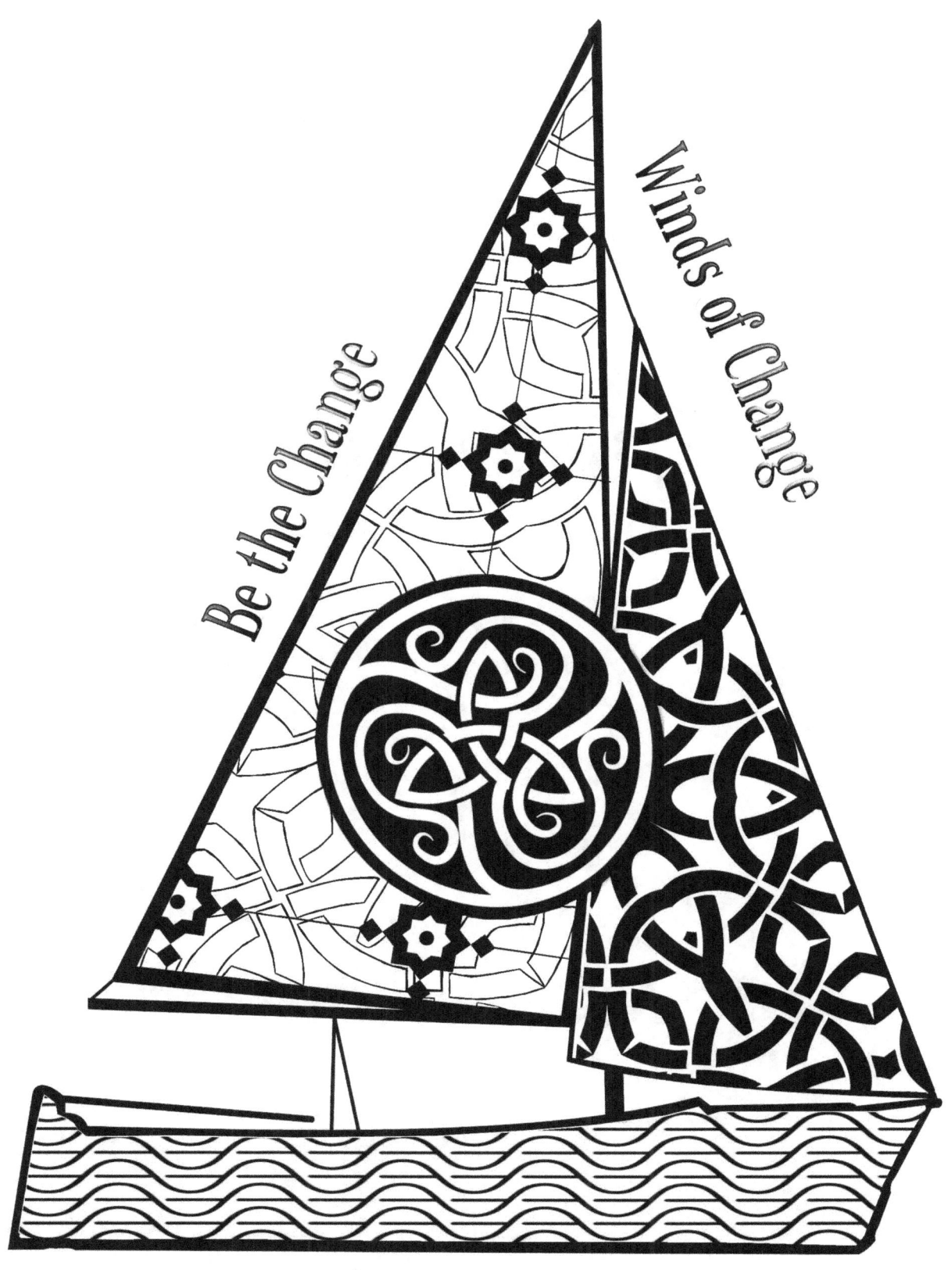

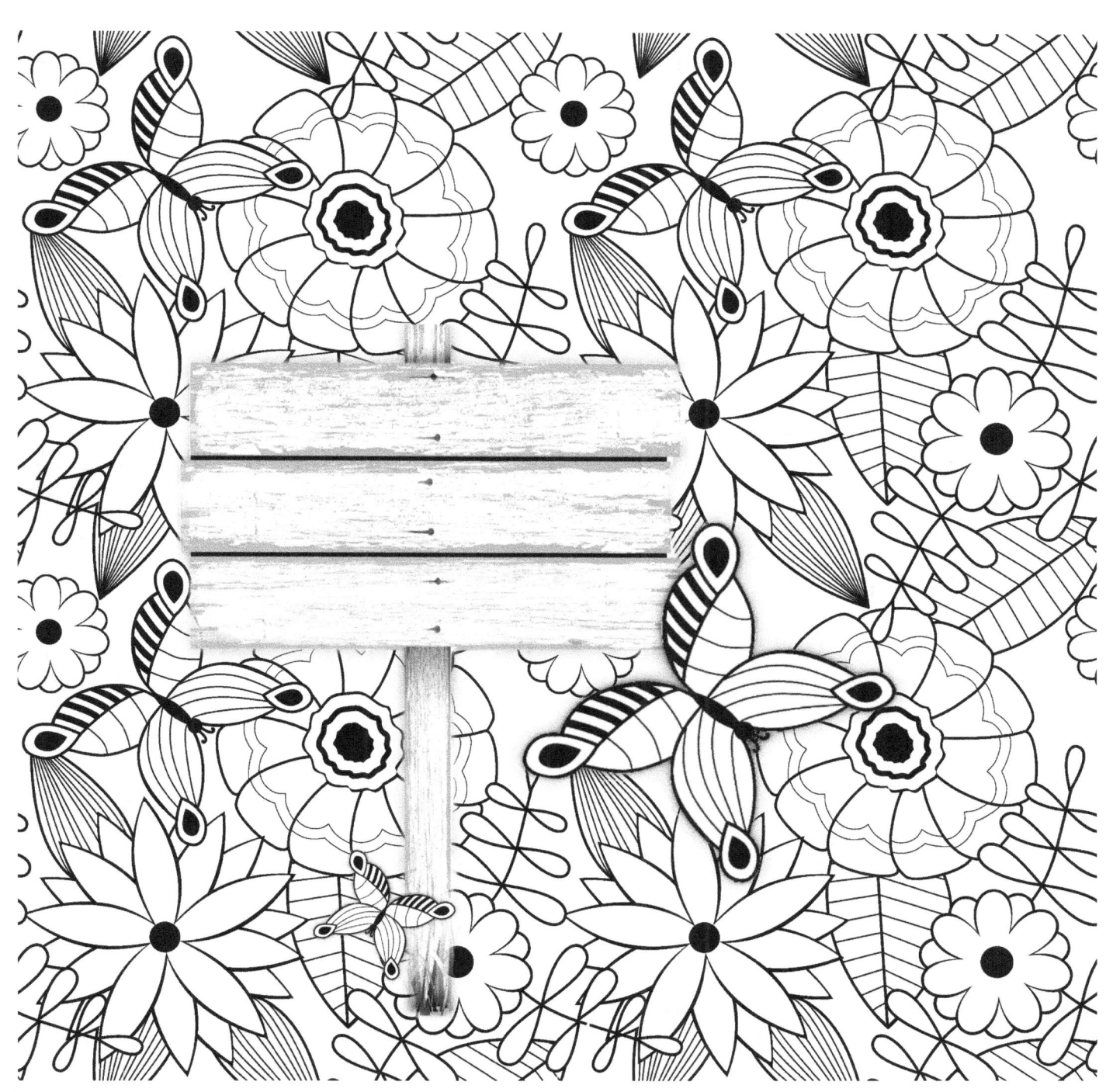

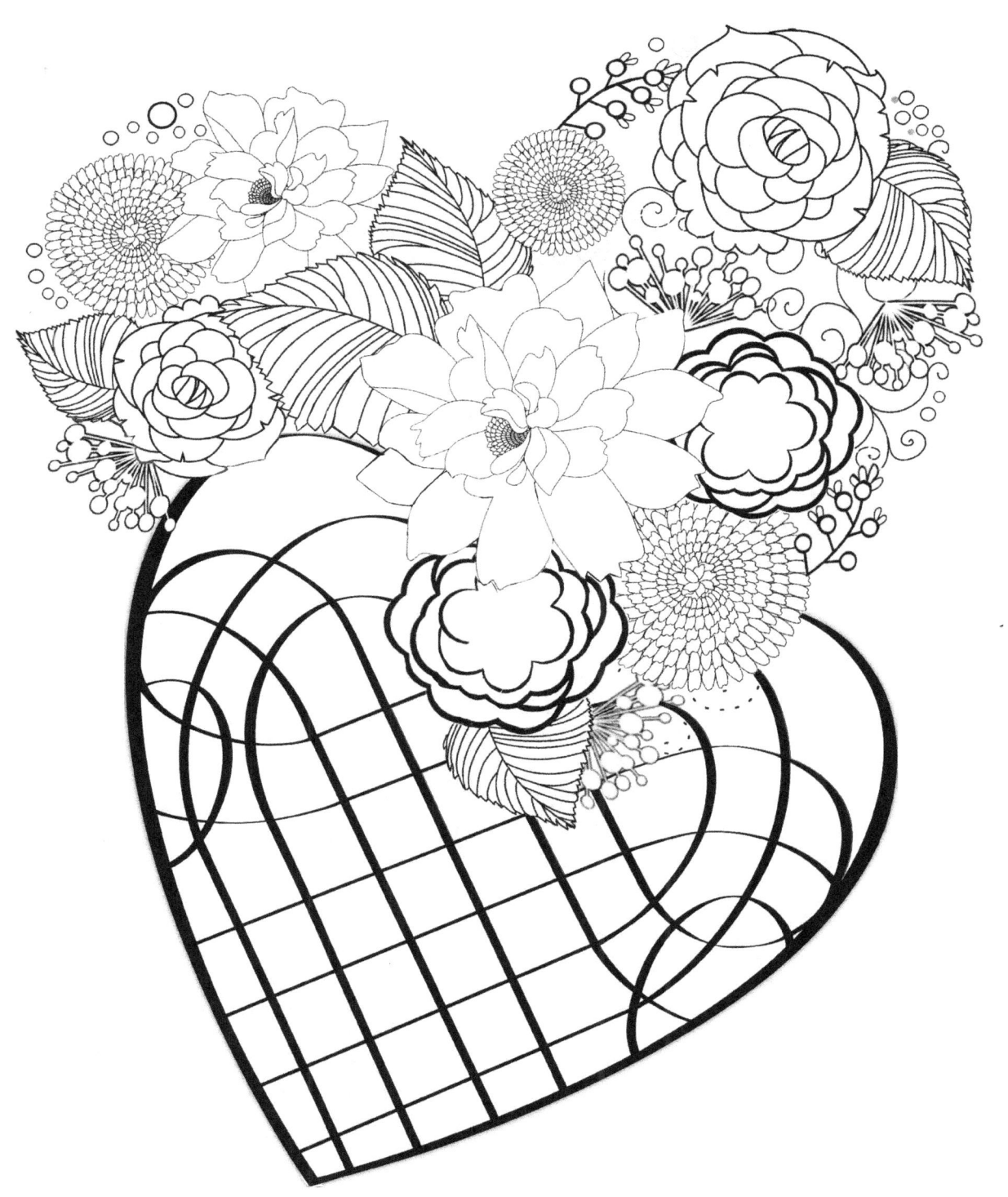

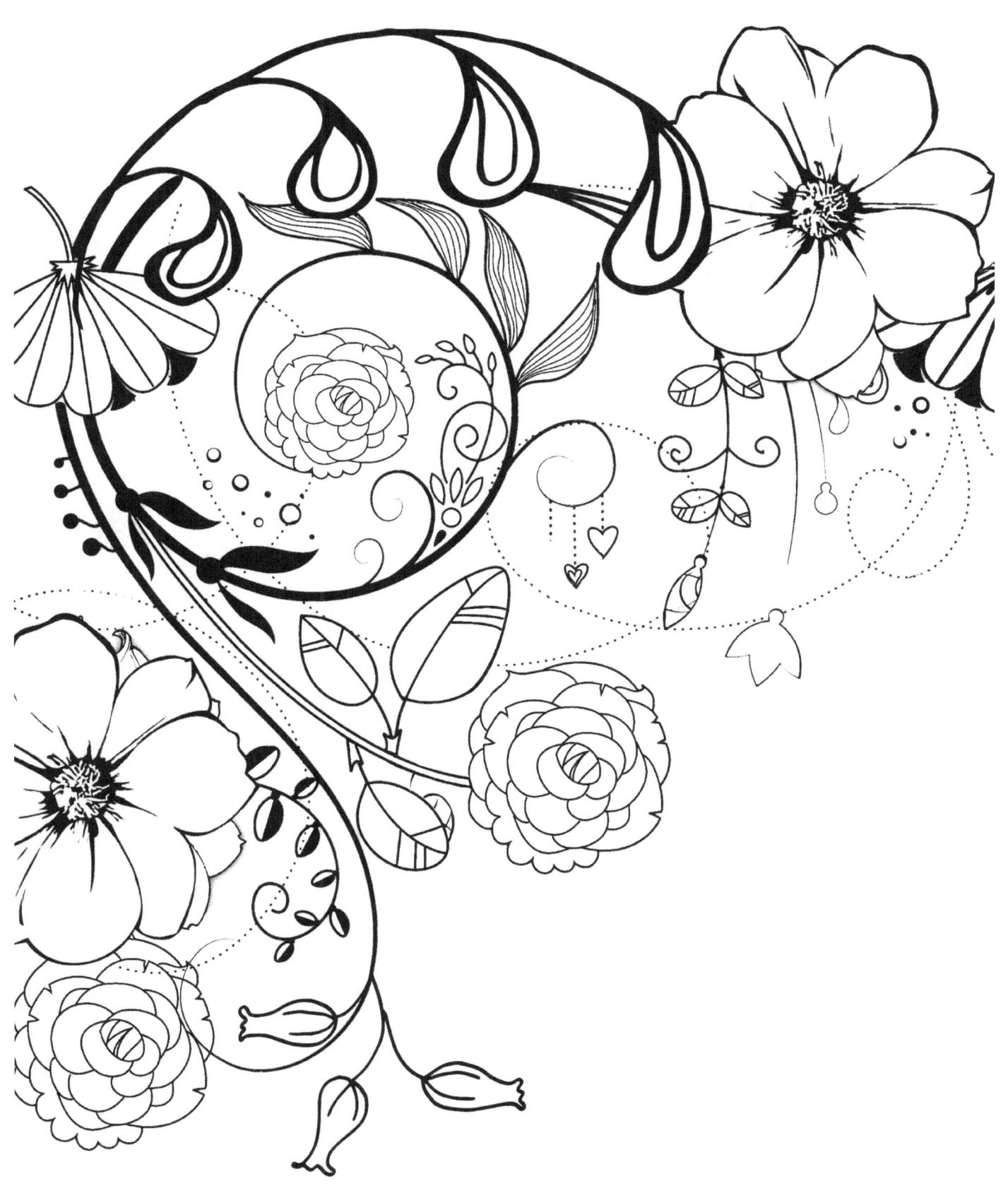

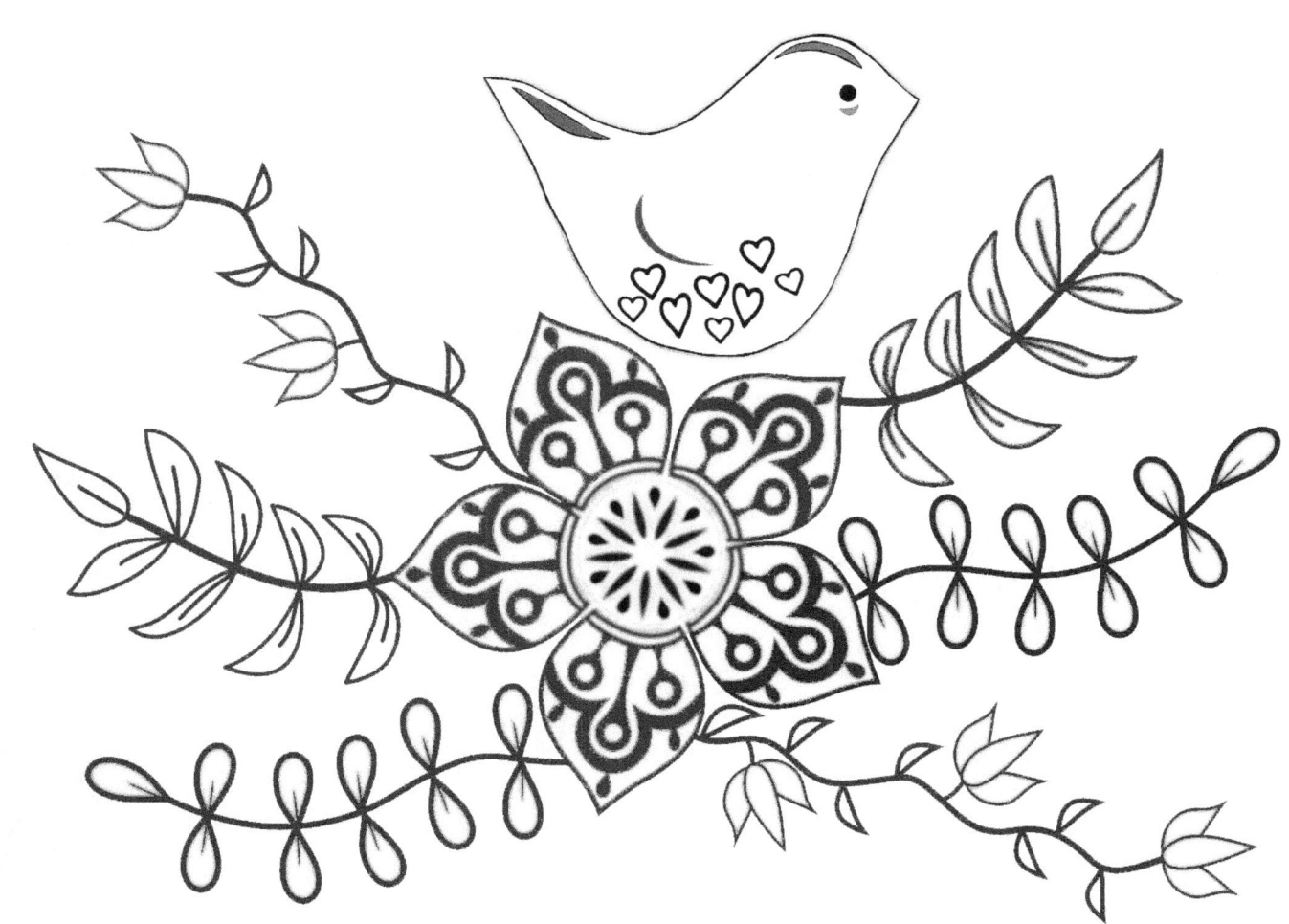

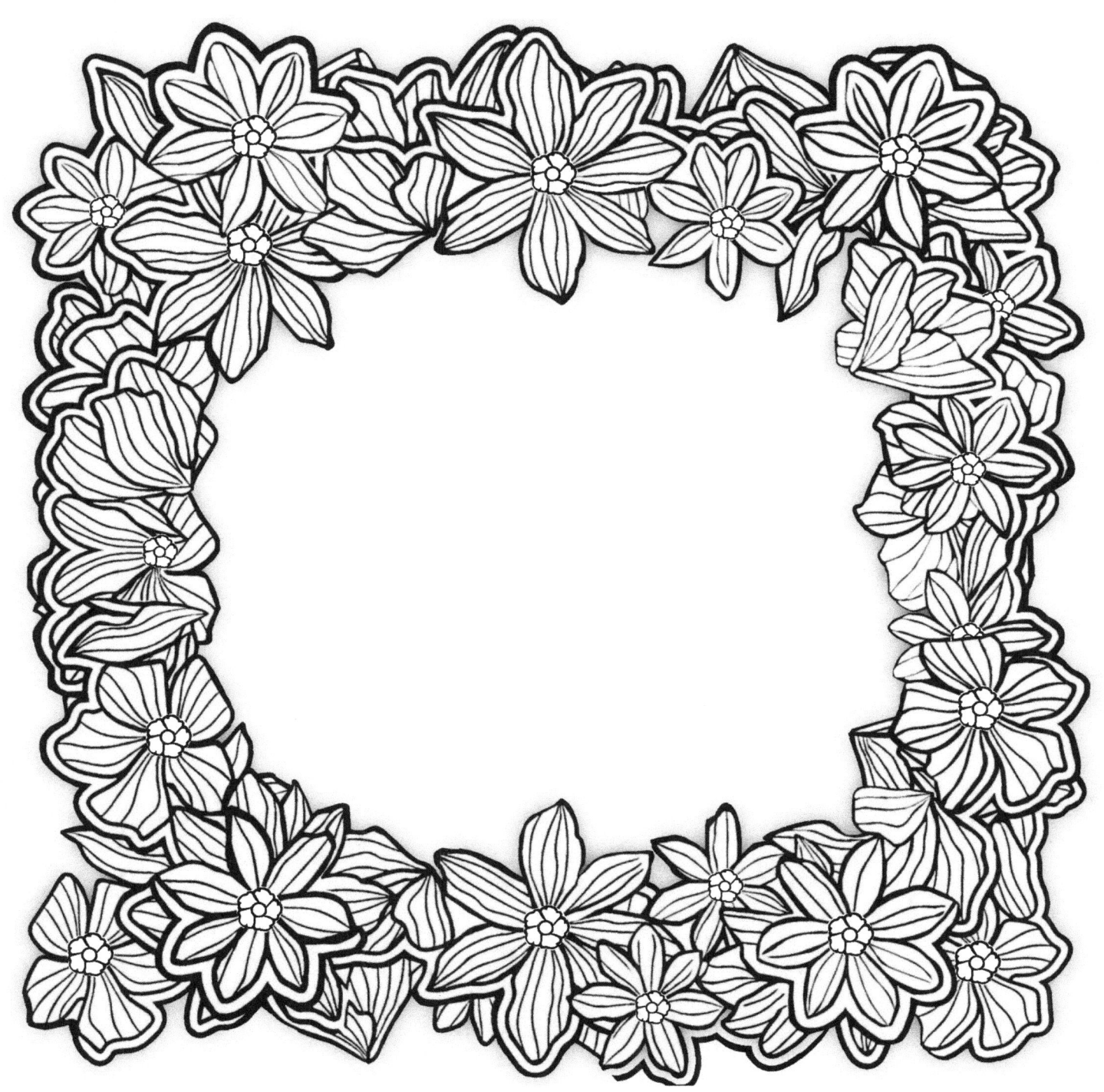

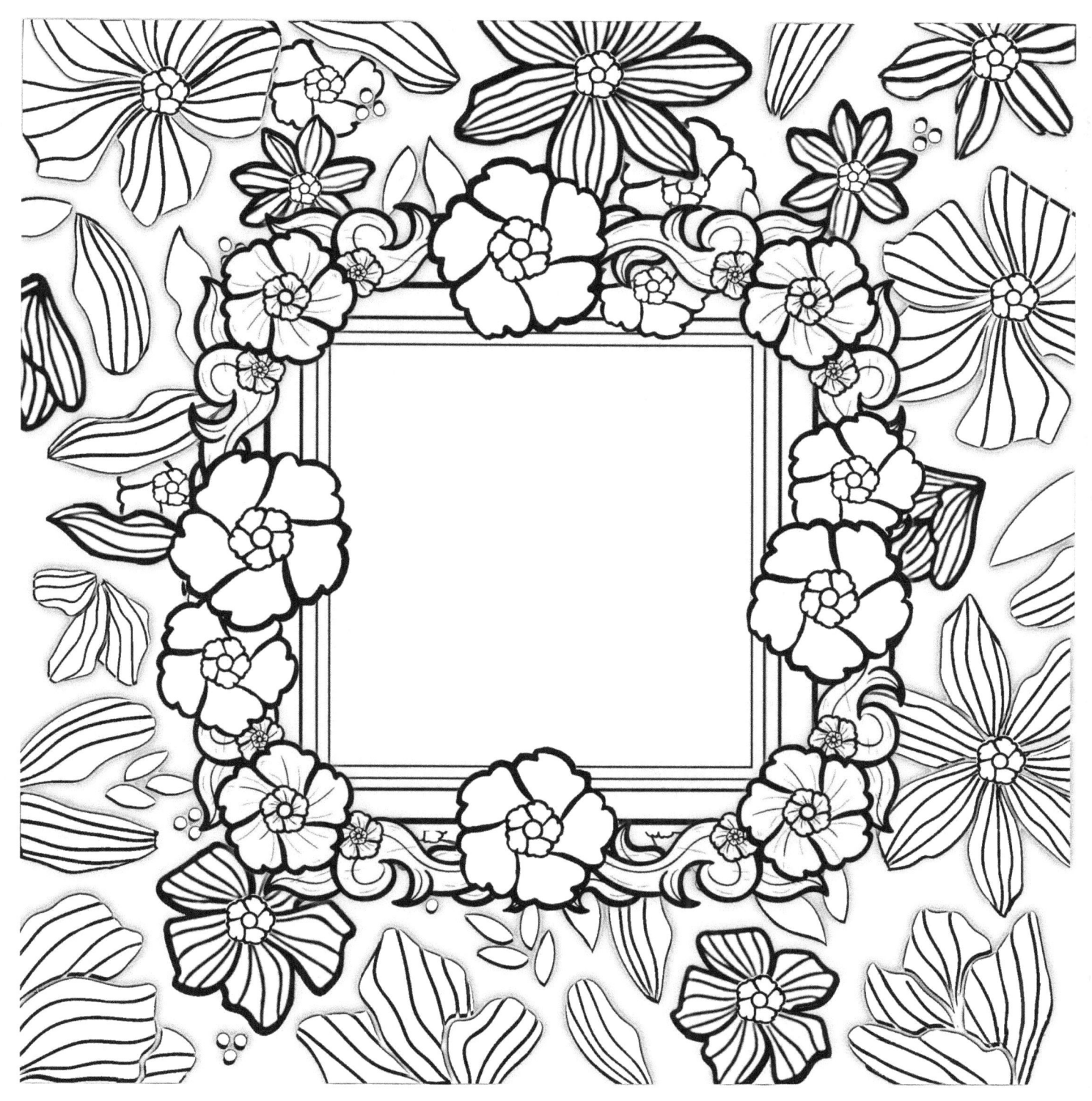

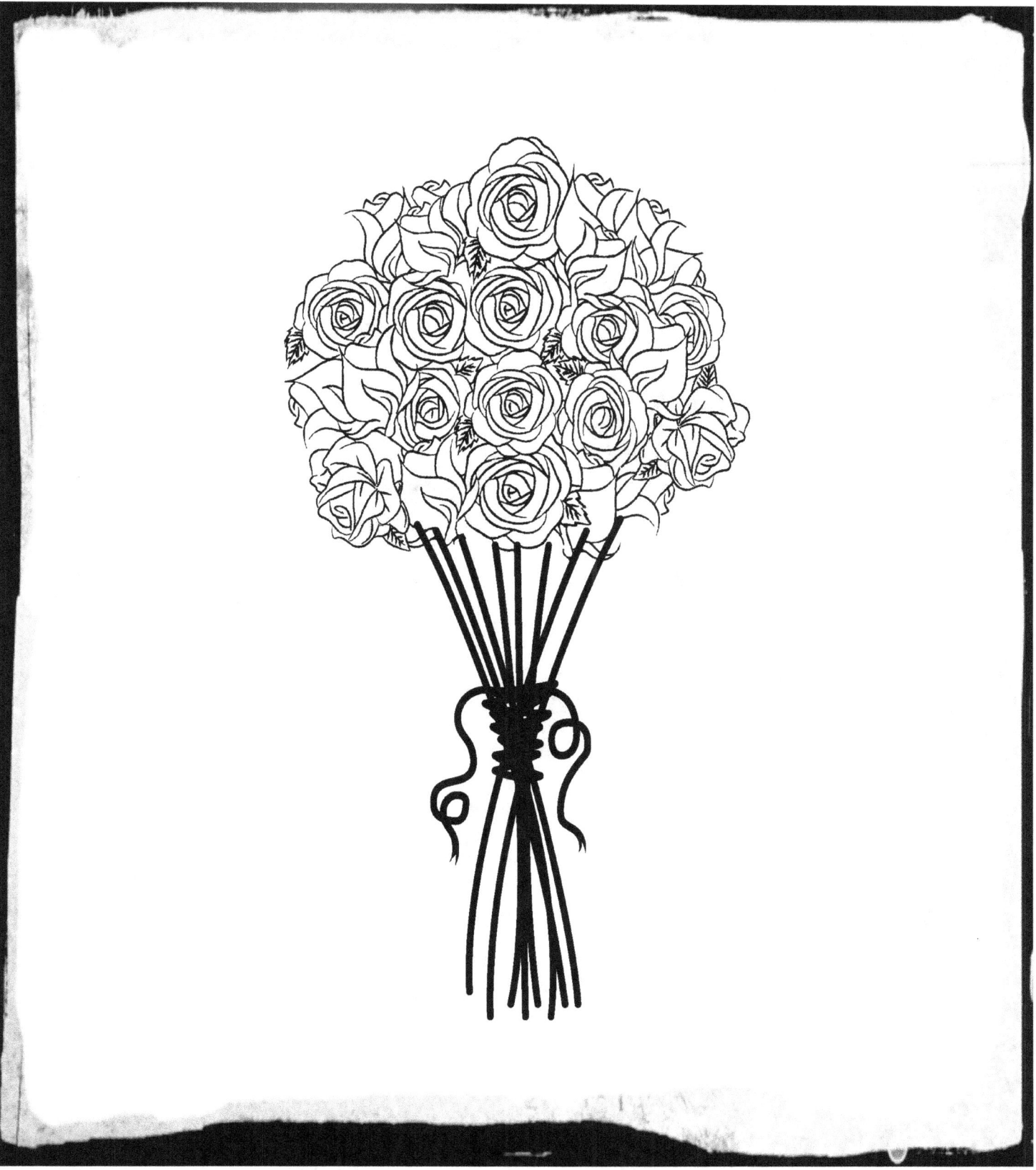

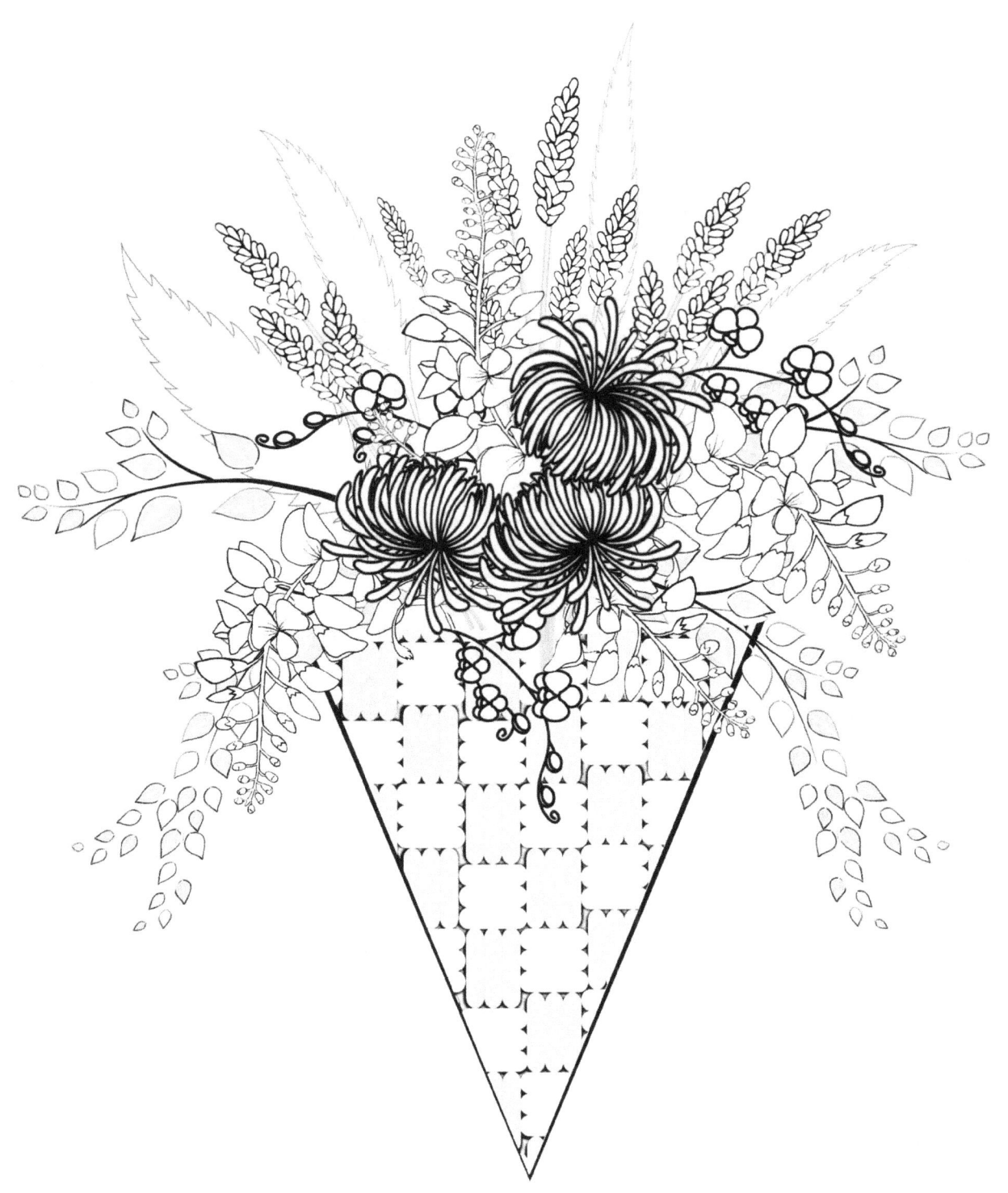

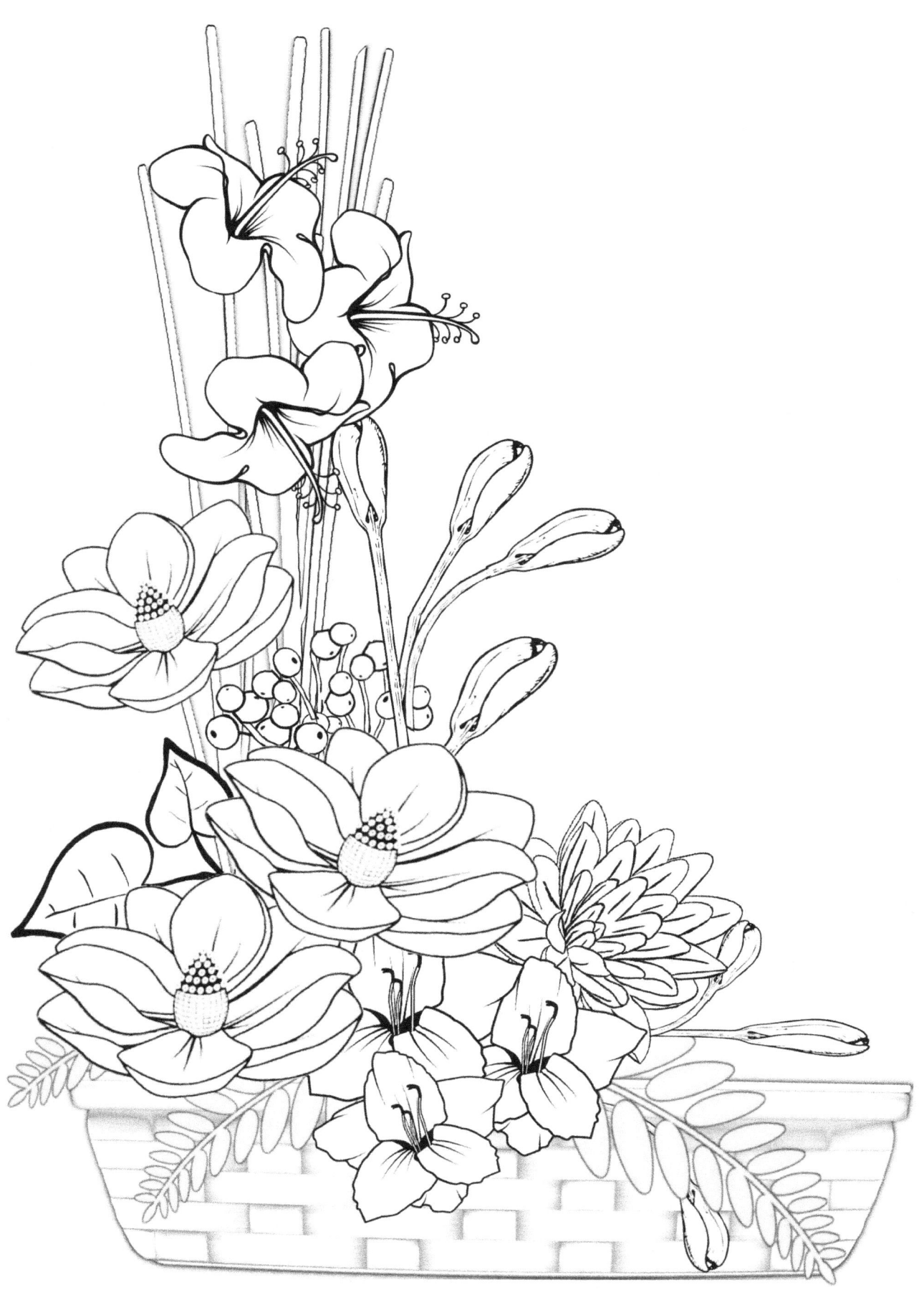

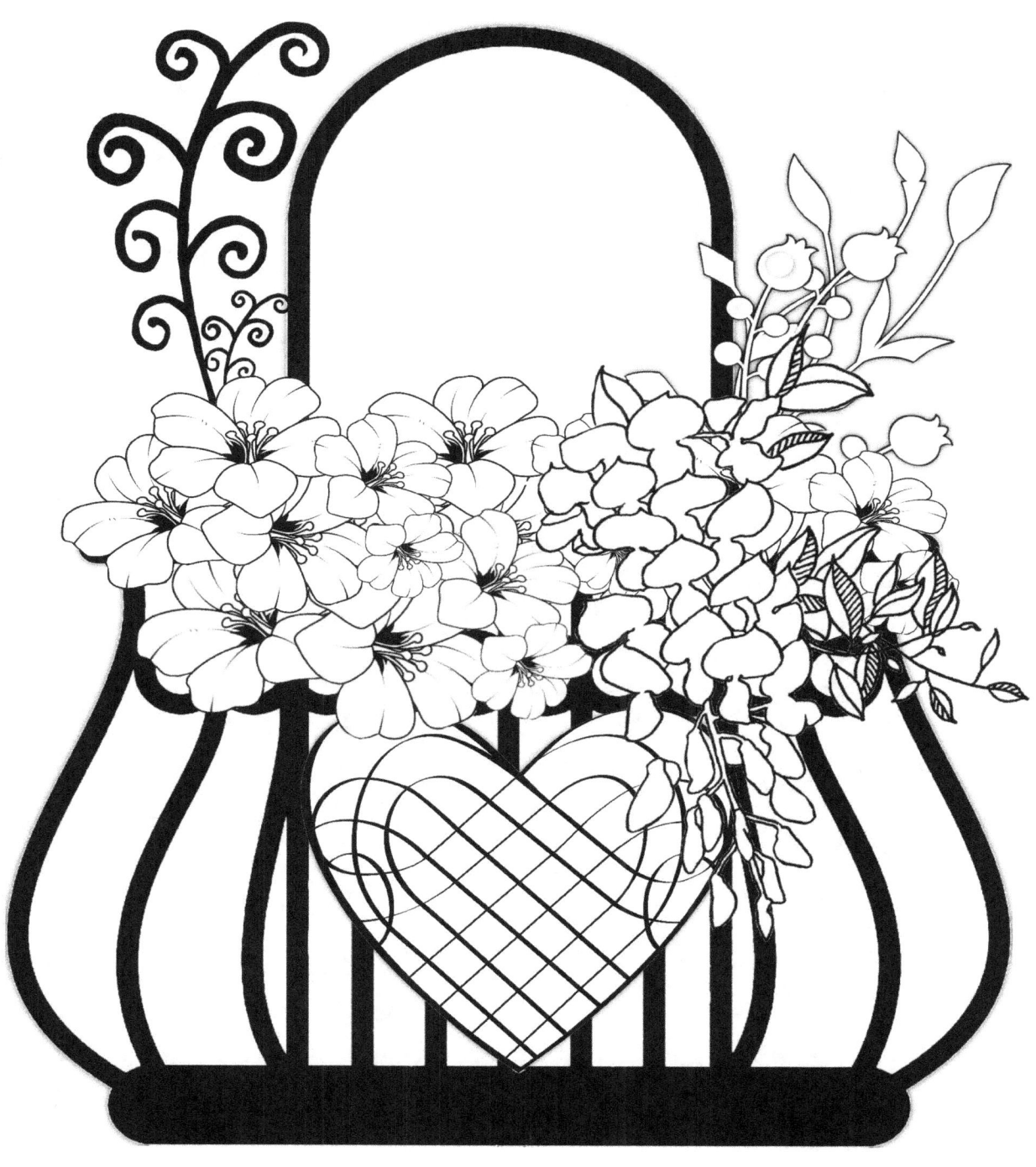

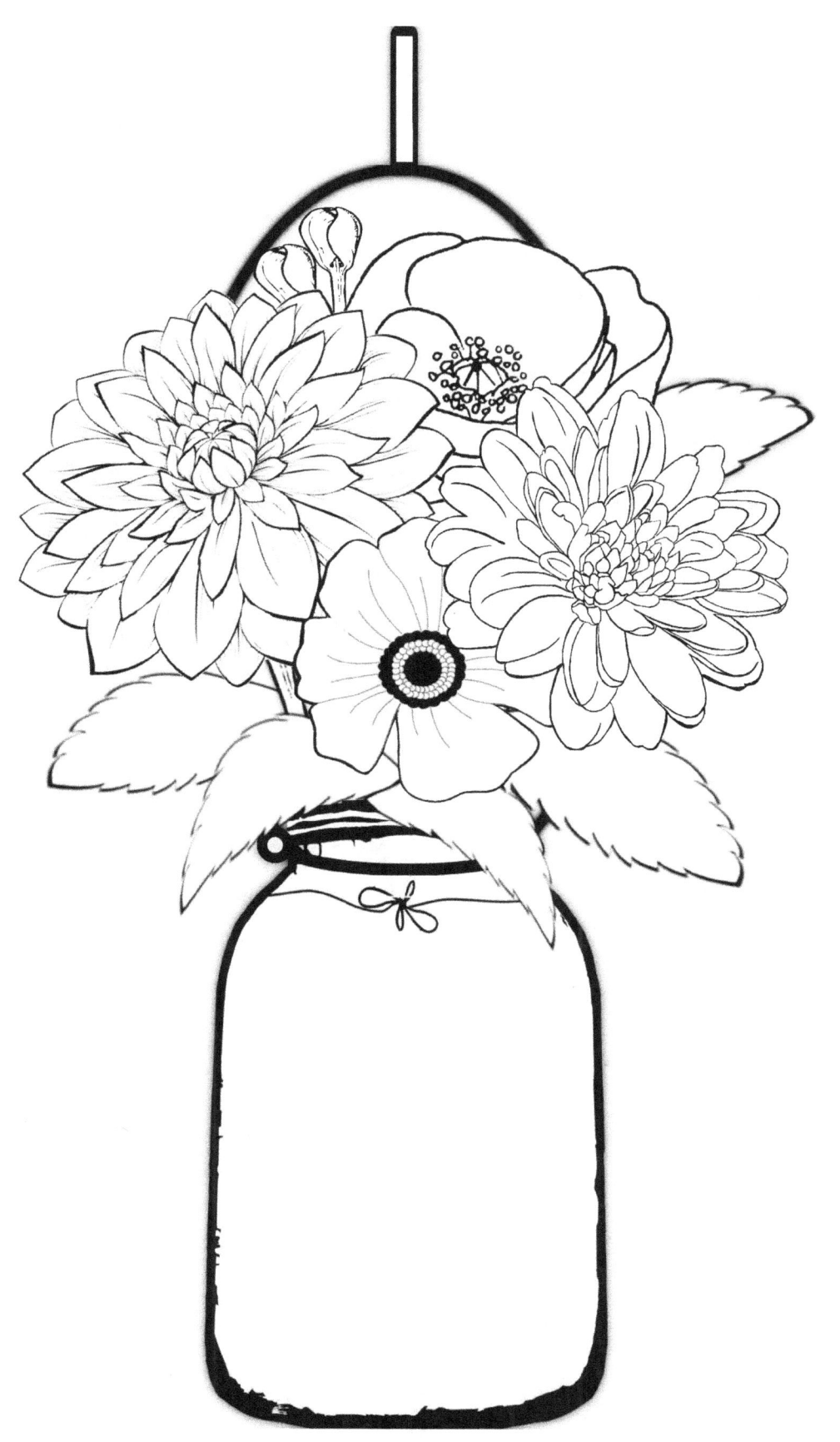

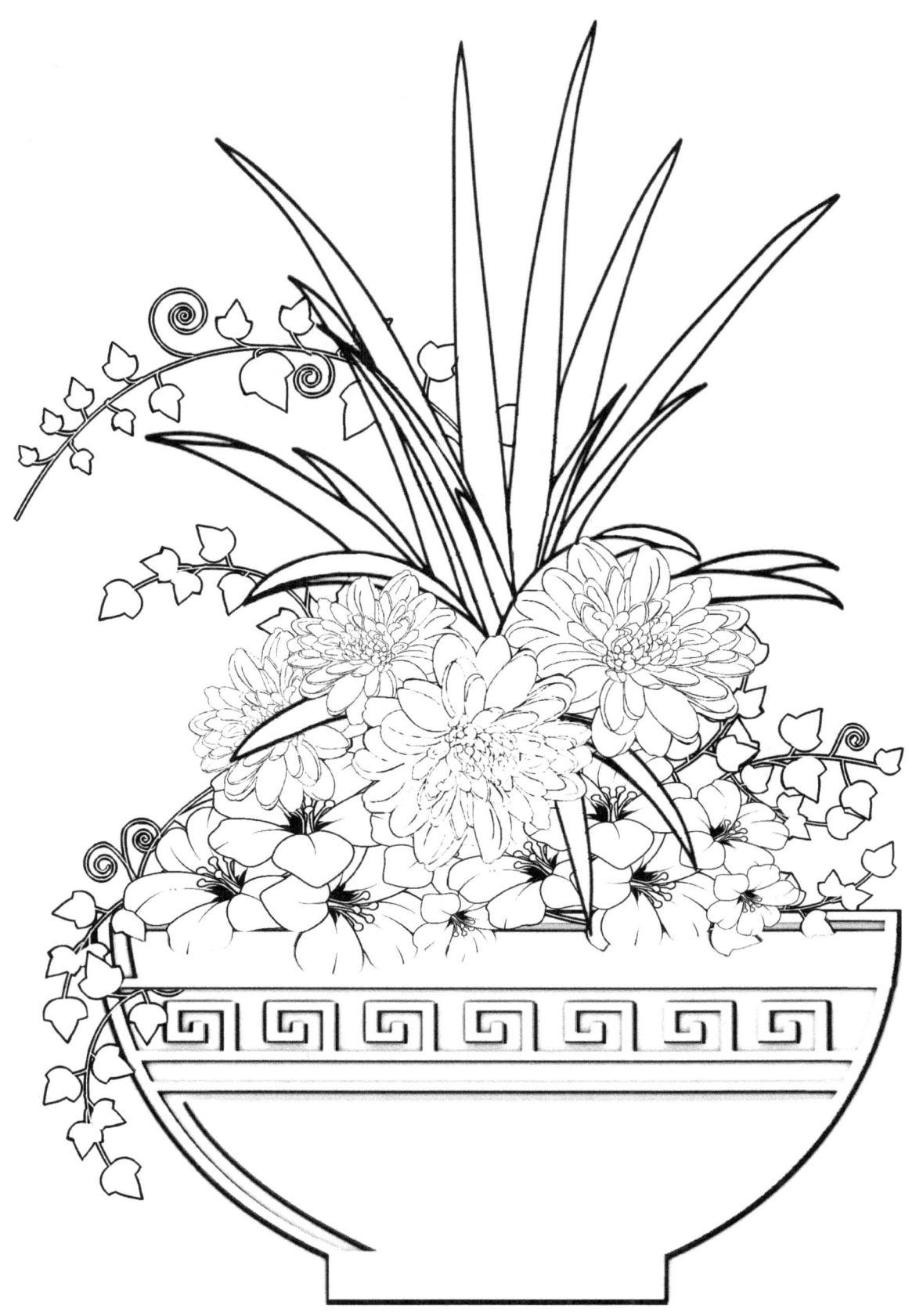

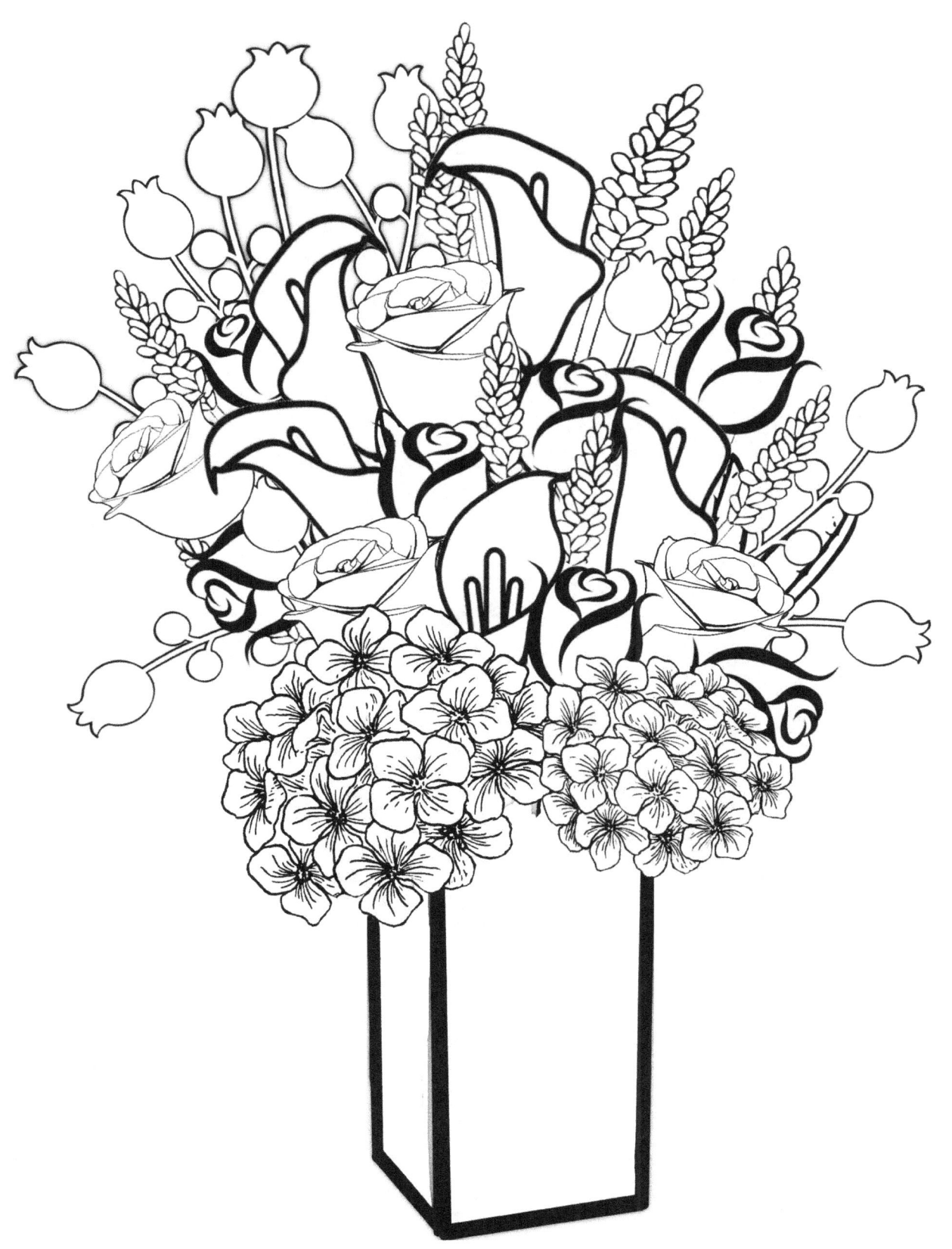

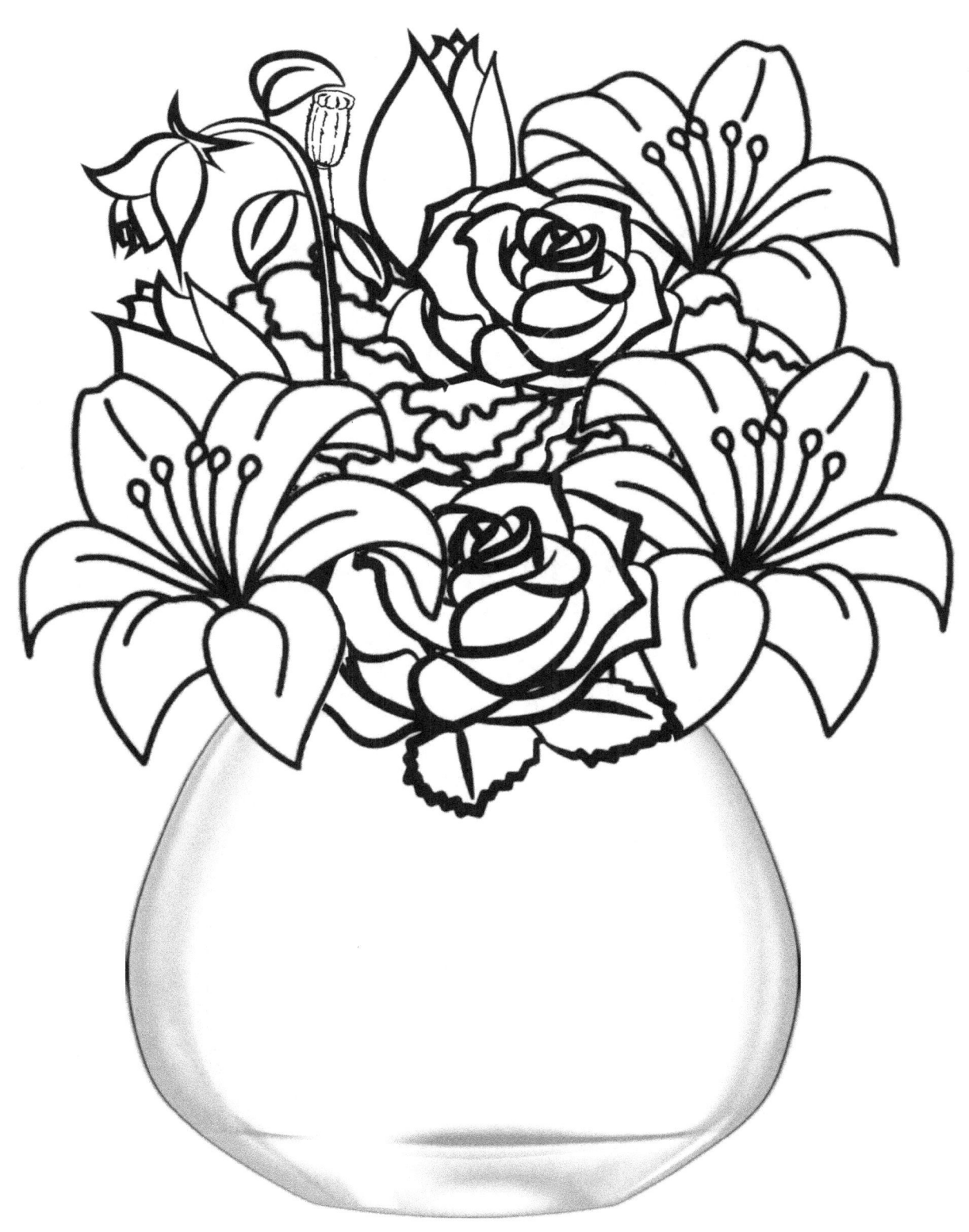

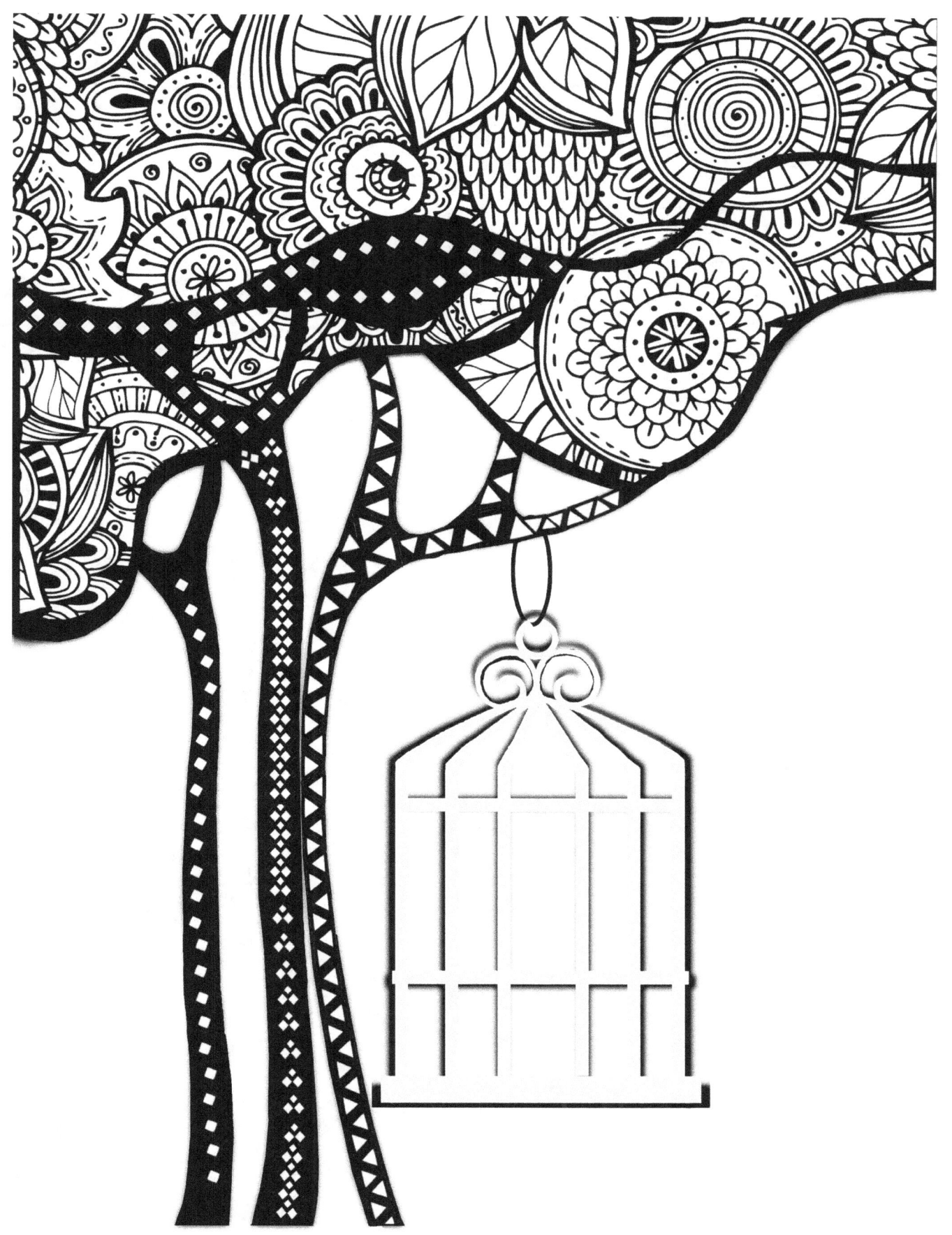

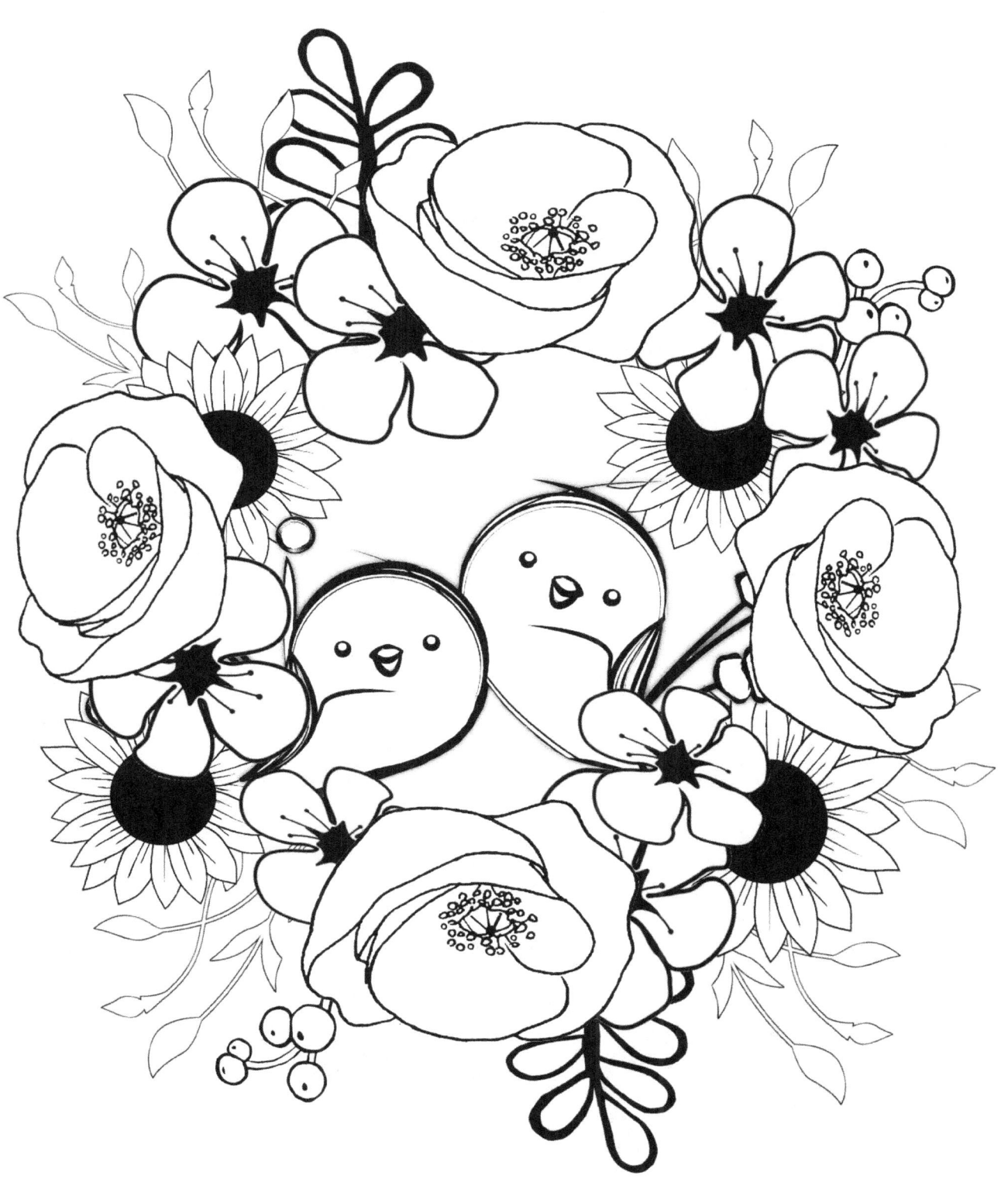

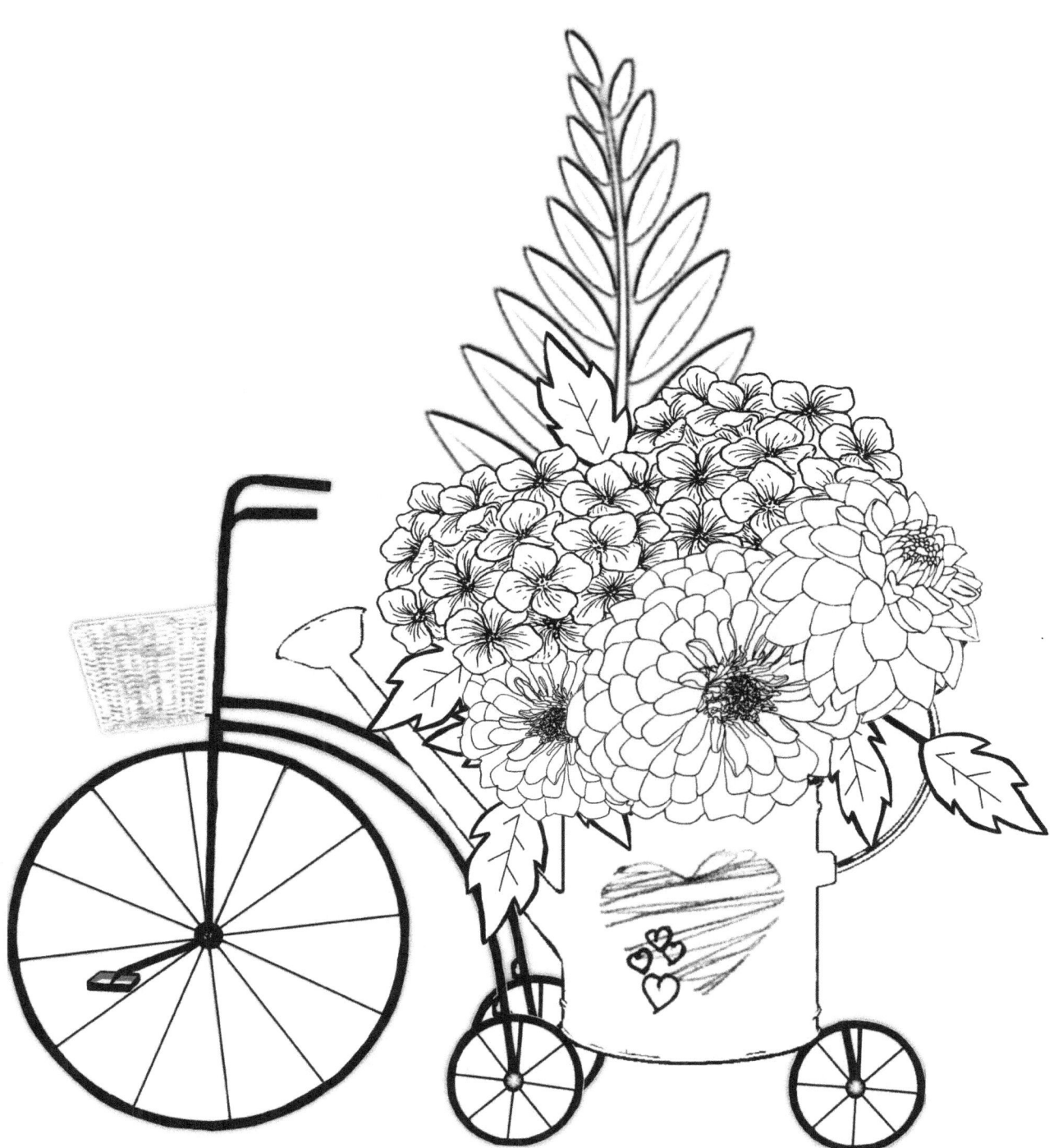

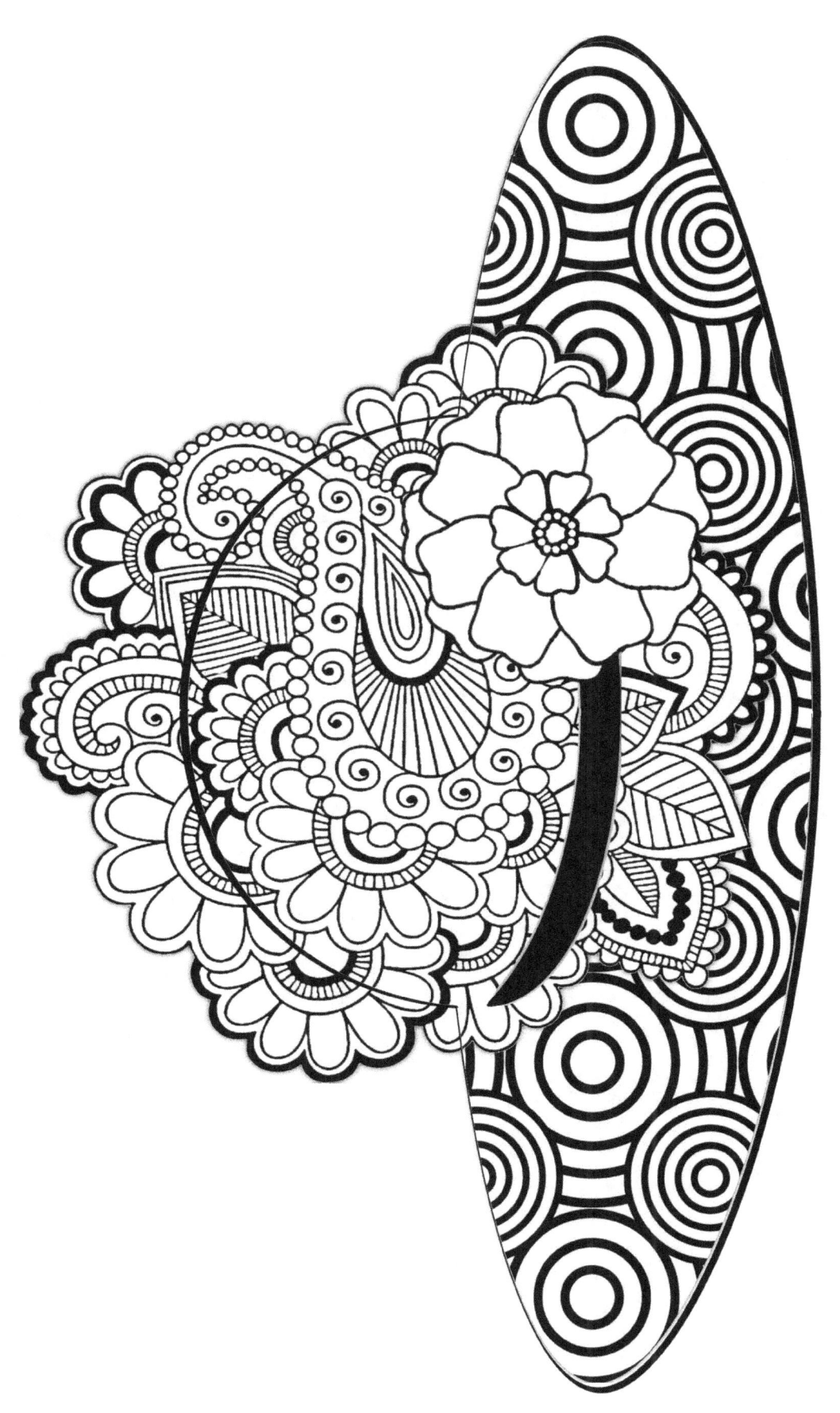

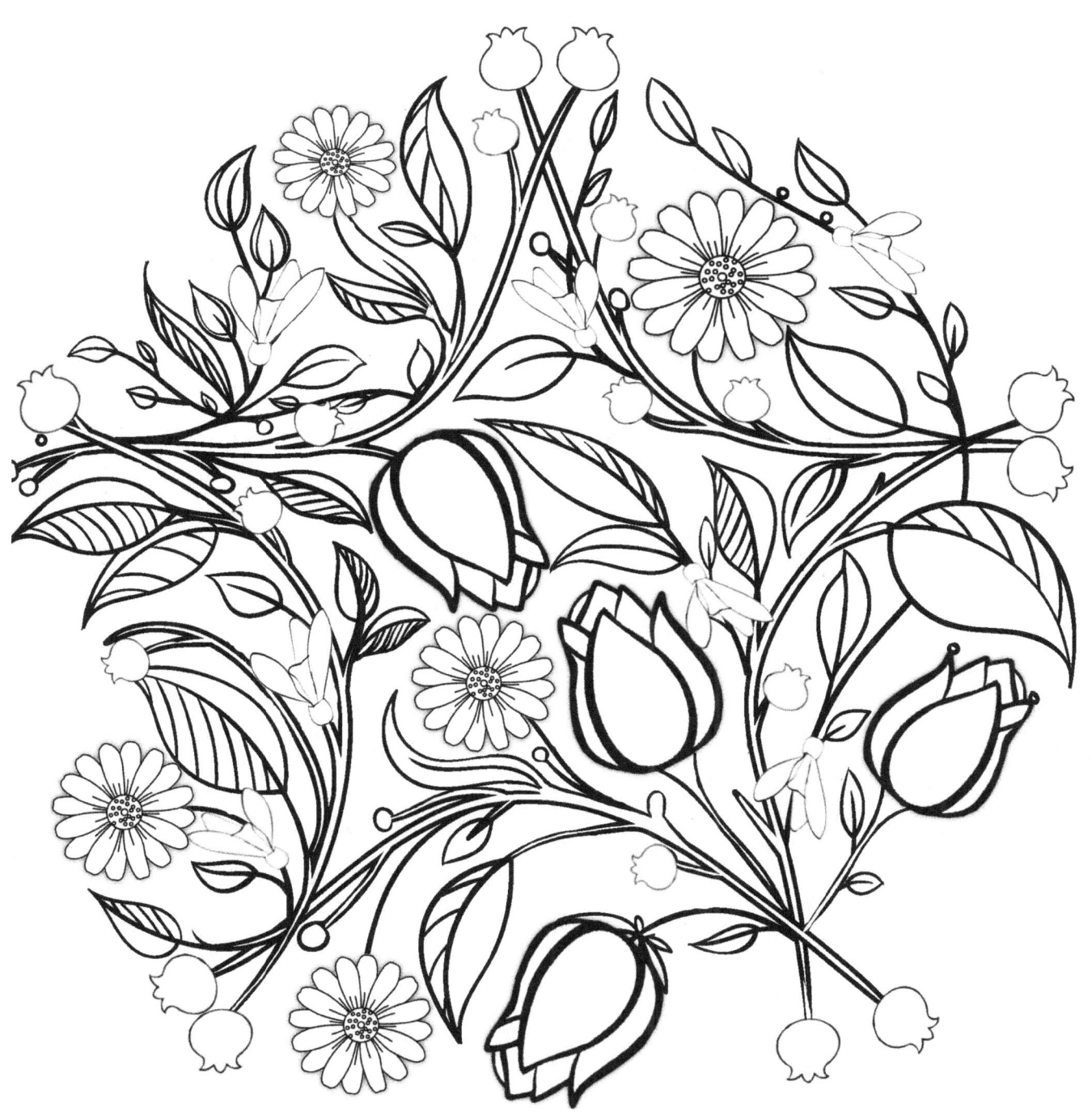

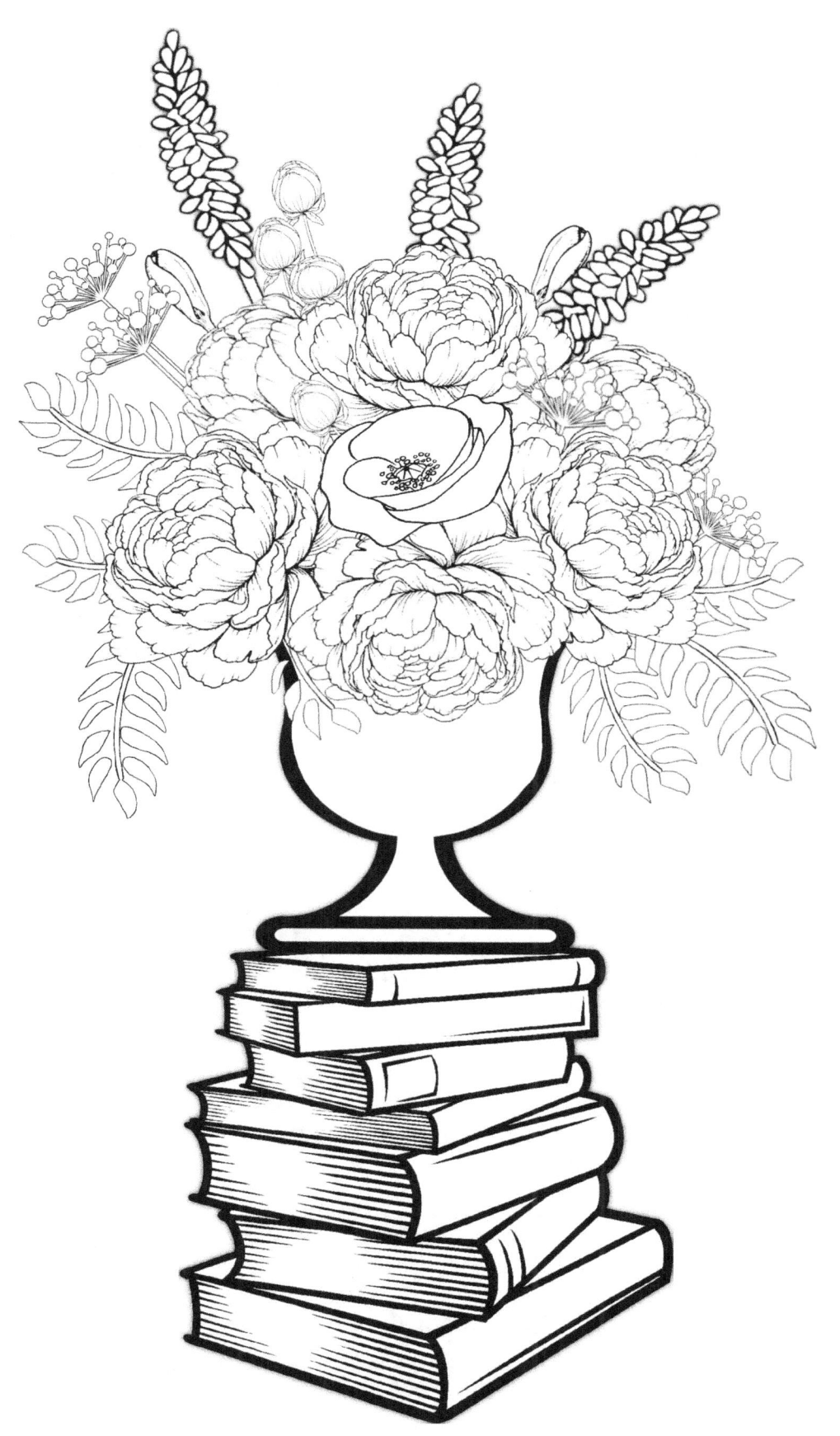

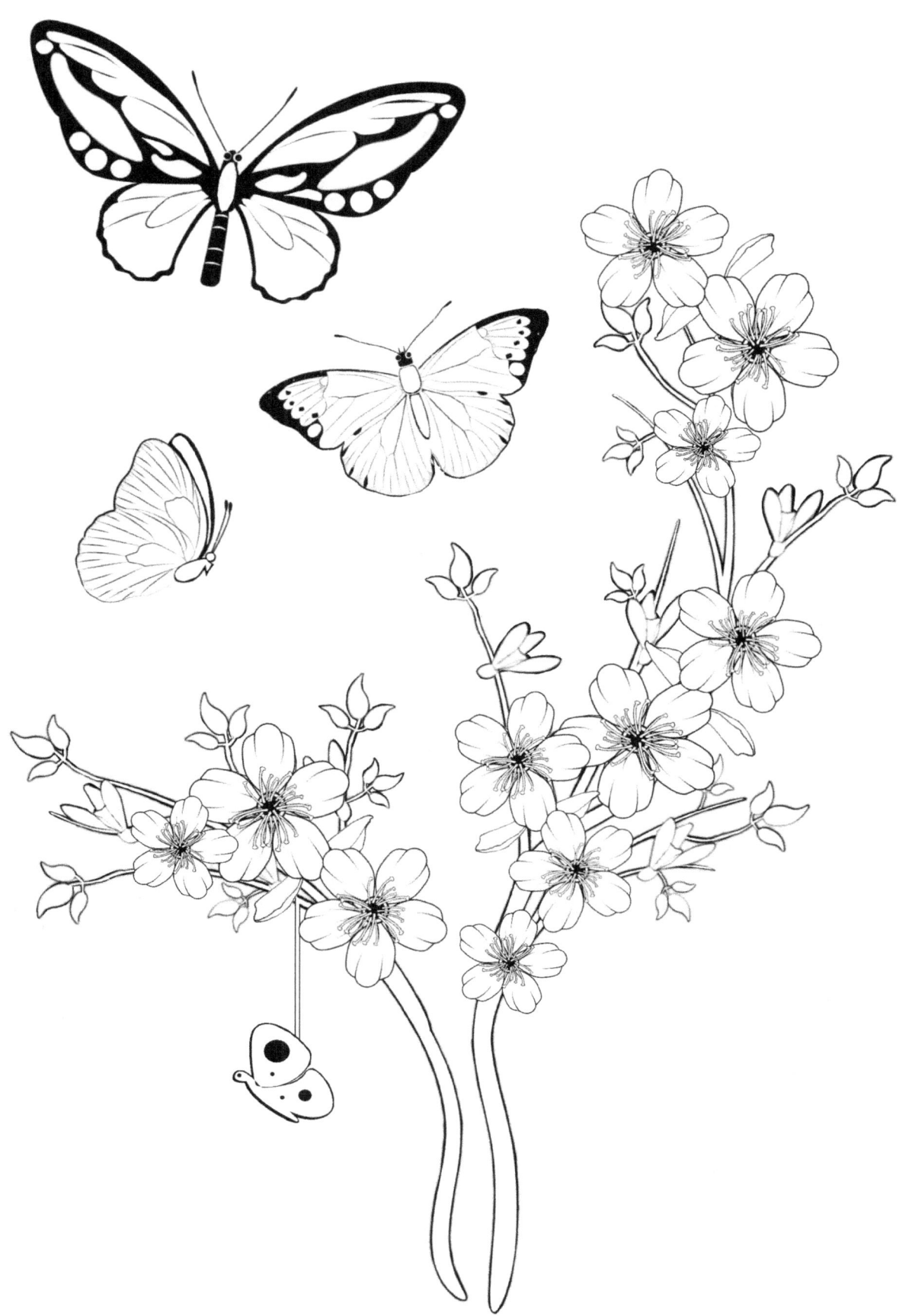

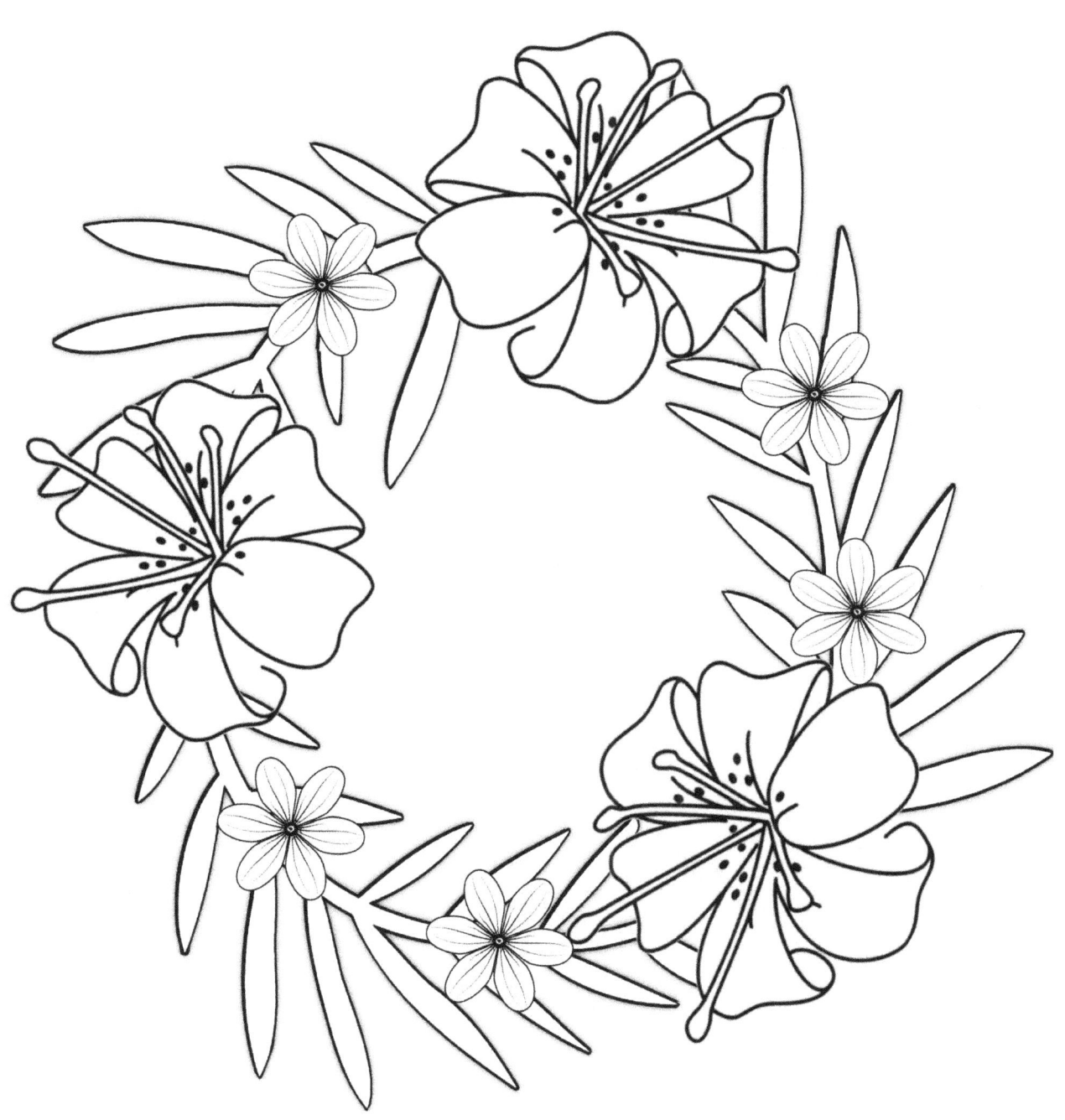

About the Author

I was born, and raised in the beautiful Appalachian Mountains on the East Coast in Maryland. And have 2 teenage sons...Jake and Luke. It is because of them I work so hard, and dedicate so much time – in the area of emotional health. I think most of us who have children become more aware of our surroundings after they're born. Most specifically the environment and global warming. We try and do better to take care of it as best as we can. For me, it's mental health [although I recycle too:] as it negatively affects both sides of our family, and deeply. But it's a worldwide problem too. I'm well versed in this area and on many levels - so for the past 15 years, I've dedicated my life to contributing to mental awareness, self-help, suicide prevention, healing and the methods of. Not just for me & my family...but for all in need of emotional stability. I'm certified in Color Theory - and in what I call a perfect storm, I'd combined my education with my life experiences and began "YourAdvoKit." A community for all those in need of a friend and support. And I will spend the rest of my life supporting and helping those in need of emotional support. It's my passion; and it's been an honor. Because it takes a village, and if you'll allow me to be a part of yours...I'm in! – Hugs, Susan

The Buck Doesn't Stop Here!

Download FREE and fun resources, life hacks, printables, quotes and guides that help improve your quality of life & promote a healthy mind - all while living your life less stressed at **YourAdvoKit.com**

Bundles for Enhancing Your Mental Health Including:

- The Law of Attraction for Easing Depression
- The Emotional Freedom Technique [EFT] or Tapping
- Meditation for Easing Depression
- Mindfulness and Mental Health

Life Hack/Tip Sheets Including:

Procrastination | Never Give Up | Be More Open Mind | Simplify Your Life | Spirituality | Be More Outgoing | Motivation | Become More Giving | Embrace Discipline | Exude Confidence

Getting the Girl: Compassionate, real life, relationship advice. "Getting the Girl" is a beautifully written publication while maintaining an honest balance of respect and truth. While written for men, the advice can be applied to all...as manners, respect, kindness and love have no boundaries and should be shared and given in abundance no matter the technicalities.

Goal Setting Information and Downloadable Infographic

Coloring Books

More "Hue Knew?" Coloring Books

Not everyone uses coloring books to ease depression, soothe anxiety or boost self-esteem. But for those who do, and because with all my heart I want to make a difference, even if it is just a small contribution...I've also a set of affirmation cards that compliment this coloring book and its theme for download and they are yours FREE! They are beautifully done in the same color scheme as this coloring book and are the size of a business card for your convenience; to be laminated, cut and carried with you and read daily until the affirmation truly resonates.

They're on the same page as the color swatch I mentioned at the beginning of this book.

Enjoy!